OMG

Oh My Gosh, What I See, Feel, and Hear Now

Richard Mitchell

Fulton Books
Meadville, PA

Published by Fulton Books 2023

ISBN 979-8-88731-143-2 (paperback)
ISBN 979-8-88731-144-9 (digital)

Printed in the United States of America

Hi, my name is Richard Mitchell. Just call me Ricky; that's what my family and friends call me. I just celebrated the tenth anniversary of my stroke and brain surgeries, just before my sixty-first birthday.

My life really started in 1966 when I was lost, then I saw her walking in my TV English class, a petite little blond that I had never seen before, and oh, she was sitting close to Tommy Miller and Ricky Miles. I go to grade sheets on the bulletin board; looks like her name is Sue Meyer. The next day, as Sue walks by my desk, I say, "Hi, Sue."

She comes to an immediate stop, walks back to me, and says, "How do you know my name?"

I say, "I'm clairvoyant, I can read your mind." The beginning of a beautiful life. We started dating, then on May 5, 1968, on Sue's birthday, I asked her father, Frank, if I could have Sue for my wife. On May 2, 1969, we married, and three days later, Sue celebrated her birthday. Nine days later, I celebrated my birthday. Then on May 24, 1969, we graduated from high school, and next, on June 3, 1969, we moved to Winter Park, Florida, but in July, we moved to Maitland, Florida.

Now the draft wants me for the Vietnam War. Oh, oh, Sue becomes pregnant, and now the draft is not interested anymore. Sue was a little scared there in Maitland, so we moved back to Winter Park, about half a mile from her mom, dad, and her little sisters. We stayed in Winter Park until the boys were born and moved to Pine Hills, where we stayed. So on May 12, 1970, labor began, and we rushed to the hospital. Then my wife's doctors now conspire to drive me crazy; one says she is in labor, while the other says her chemistry is wrong and is not in labor.

Finally, on my birthday, May 14, they decided to take x-rays to see what was wrong. When I saw the doctor looking at the x-rays, I told Sue, "They are going to tell us you have twins." After four days of labor, Sue had to go cesarean; Sue's specialist didn't know how to perform an emergency cesarean, and we need surgeon to perform the cesarean. The doctor that was found does the cesarean and delivers the twins (identical). Sue's scar is seven inches long and two inches wide, vertically raised about a quarter inch. Three years later, when our daughter was born, Sue tried to go natural but couldn't get hard enough contractions, so our new surgeon repaired her uterus. He told us that her uterus was torn up.

I found a job on June 6, 1969, as a janitor at John H. Harland check printers. By 1975, I had learned everything about letterpress operations. By August 1975, I was no. 6 in the plant of 100, then I found out how this happened, and I had trumped up charges against me. I couldn't work there anymore, but they had a job for me in Rochester, New York, or Puerto Rico. Then I put application for Walt Disney World but started to work at Air Flow AC until Disney called me on December 11, 1975.

Ralph Kent, the artist in charge of copyright art, hired me because he needed a numbering expert for the project to stop ABCDE tickets and start printing passports for admission into the Magic Kingdom. The first month I saved the company $40,000, and I asked, "What do I get?"

The answer to a handshake is *a job*. I stayed until August 26, 1986, when my boss decided to promote his buddy to the supervisor job over tickets. I told the supervisor what I thought, and he told me, "There is a door over there and another over there. Pick one, and don't let it hit you on the *a*———on the way out!" I took door no. 2. I went to another print shop until work ran out. On May 23, 1989, I returned to Walt Disney World as a teamster like my father as a truck driver. Being the learner that I have always been, I became a forklift trainer, tour guide for Disney Institute, member of the cast advisory council, adopt a shop, assistant scuba instructor, and now a member of Golden Ears Club.

Why am I in the Golden Ears Club?

The Beginning!

On October 8, 2010, Friday morning, when I was going to work, oops! This white Toyota? Why is it pacing this car in front of me? Good, the car in front of me is getting in the right lane so I can pass it. What? I'm on the wild teacup ride at Disney! The Toyota lost control and hit me. Now that I have had time to think it out, this gentleman from Haiti has lost control of his car, saw he was going to hit my car, and hit the brakes, but oops, it was the gas. Lucky for him, he missed the northbound traffic and ended up on the sidewalk, not so lucky for me and my wife. We spun out of control into the median and, alas, into the subdivision wall. Ouch, dazed and confused, I'm looking at the wall six inches outside my car window. When the fire department rescue shows up, they want to get the jaws of life to get me out. I say, "*No*, I will move the car forward," and they say it won't work, but I moved it forward, ouch!

The paramedic asks me, "Can you move?"

I tell him, "Maybe if you help me, but please have your backboard ready because my back, legs, and feet are hurting, and I do not know how long I can stand."

I stood for about one minute when my legs started to buckle. The paramedic caught me with the backboard just in time. The next thing I know, I'm on the gurney, pushed into the ambulance, and we start moving.

I asked, "Where is my wife?"

I was told that she stayed at the accident. "What? She is injured also," I said.

The trip was short. After minutes, I was pushed into the emergency room hallway, and somebody took my BP, 165/95. I was in a daze but thought it was normal for a trauma. Next to the x-ray to check my neck and lower back. The emergency room doctor said that I had no broken bones and that everything was okay. Oops, why are my feet, legs, and lower back still hurting? The doctor says, "Let's do an MRI on the lower back." The doctor found trauma in the lower back.

I get a lawyer; he lines me up with therapy to try and get me in shape to work again. Unfortunately, I'm hurt too much. I'm going through therapy, and my father was having complications with his cancer, causing pneumonia. The doctors say that they have found that my father's intestines have a blockage and need an operation. Fortunately, when they make the incision, his intestines untangle. But within the week, on October 27, 2010, my father passed from pneumonia. I was present when he passed. Just prior to his passing, he asks where that door behind his bed went because he keeps seeing these people going in and out of it. There was a wall with no door visible, but I could feel the door was there. Within minutes, my father passed, and I could feel and see his spirit rise up out of his body and shoot through that door behind his bed, passing the angels lined up in there. It was a streak of light into light.

After six weeks of going through therapy, I get headaches and got an MRI of the brain. Oops, my neurologist told me that the therapy was over till I took care of that, and he was pointing at the right side of my head. I have a tumor in my brain! He recommends a neurosurgeon. I get a second opinion from my nephew, who is a doctor in radiology. Yes, my nephew says, "You have a meningioma the size of a walnut, and it is putting pressure on the brain, you've been having pains in your head?"

I say, "About twice a month for two or three seconds, it felt like somebody stuck a hat pin through my head."

He says, "That's the tumor. Have you laughed for no reason, cried for no reason, or gotten mad for no reason?"

I said, "Immediately for about the last thirty years. I've been getting mad for no reason."

He says immediately, "I was about to tell you that it had been there for a long time from the looks of the tumor, and maybe, removal would be good, easy to get at, and should be no problem."

The neurosurgeon recommends the same thing. On January 25, 2011, removal of the tumor, I remember seeing the inside the hole in my head and seeing the red, bluish-gray looks similar to cauliflower, but I see a dent on the surface about two inches long and 1/8 inches wide and deep, like when you put your fingernail into the skin type of dent. I was seeing this like I was next to the table looking in. I guess this is an out-of-body event, *wow!* On January 28, 2011, I was released from the hospital to recover at home; my grandson Justin became my sitter because he is homeschooled and can do his homework at my house, and Cassandra came over to help also.

February 3, 2011

I feel pressure inside my skull on the right forehead; I have a stroke; I saw a light and went for it. When I get to the light, it's bright and beautiful and feels like a big warm hug. What? There is no pain in my legs, feet, and toes. Next, there was a big field with a forest, so I went to it and took one step, but I heard, "Turn around, go back, it's not your time."

Then I saw an angel, and I asked the angel, "You look like Matt Peterson, only older."

He tells me, "That's the way it is here, the young become older, the older become younger. No pain, no suffering."

I say, "Oh, are the atheists going to be surprised when they see this?"

He says, "No, they do not get to see the light and see this."

In a flash, I see fire, demons all around me, and people being tortured in all kinds of ways, screaming and yelling everywhere. When I see that little old lady in the bright-flowered dress melting into the flames, screaming at the top of her lungs, I say, "Please stop this!"

Then I'm back in heaven. Matt says, "Turn around, go back, it's not your time, get *God* and *love* back in the world."

He tells me that it is *God*, not Yahweh, Jehovah, and Allah; just *God*. Matt said that *God* gave man the law when he gave it to Moses, the Ten Commandments. The law states, "Thou shall not," not okay to do a little but obey his law, and you will be by his side! I was concerned about making it to my forty-second wedding anniversary, and Matt knew my concerns and told me not to worry. I'll have at least another forty-two. So in order to make another forty-two, 60 + 42

= 102 years old and 2,011 + 42 = 2,053, I guess all those intelligent people studying the Mayan calendars are going to be wrong, haha.

On the day of my release from the stroke, I was compelled to walk over and look out the eighth-story window, and what I saw was a helicopter prop in idle rotation. It looked like shadows, but its center was inside the building across the alleyway. I thought this was rather weird, so I asked Sue (my wife) to come over to look at what I was seeing. When she looks down where it was, she says, "What?" so I think I guess it is for my eyes only. That is when I hear a little girl crying behind me to the left, but when I turn around from the window, what? I was looking at a little girl's shadow, not on the floor or wall but standing next to me, about three feet away from me. I could see the spit curling down to her shoulders; she was holding a doll in her right hand by the arm. She was wearing a sleeveless dress just above her knees, and she was crying, wanting to know where her mommy and daddy were.

Let's see; I turn back to look out the window; my wife is behind to the right, and the little girl is behind me to my left. That is when the feeling in my chest, I now understand, is the beginning of communications. I was told that the little girl had been there since 1957; her mother and father were killed instantly in the car accident that she would die from a few days later. She was flown here, and you are seeing her memories and sending her to the light. From my left side, a light appears under the stairway, and I saw her looking at it and told her, "Your mommy and daddy are over there in the light."

She walked toward the light, and when she got to the light, in a flash, she was like sucked into the light, and the light shrunk into nothing. She had found her parents again. *Wow*, that was something different. Sue says, "Who are you talking to?"

I say, "Nobody."

When I got home, that's when things really got interesting. As I was sitting on the couch, I noticed two figures across the street. Immediately I knew it was the Bonny's; they had passed in the 1970s. Mr. Bonny passed from a leg operation first, then Mrs. Bonny passed from a car accident a couple of years later. Then I saw Steve walking around his van across the street, but he passed in August of 2010.

That's when I noticed that I wasn't seeing with my eyes or hearing with my ears; all of this was being seen and heard through the heart.

February was a lot of doctor visits, light exercises, a lot of rest, and healing. It was rough because the back, neck, and shoulder injuries were making me tired all the time. I started going to bed at 10:00 p.m. On March 9, 2011, I was awoken by a pain in my left thigh on a scale from 1 to 10, and it registered a 10. When I sat up on the edge of the bed, I felt the moisture on my right forearm. I asked Sue, "Am I sweating?"

She said, "No, there is fluid coming out of this wound on the right side of your forehead."

She called my doctor the next morning, and he said to come on in. During the examination, my doctor did everything but stand me on my head, trying to get the fluids to flow with no luck. His conclusion was it was probable spinal fluids, and I was told to go home and rest.

Sue asks, "What if it happens again?"

He says, "Call me."

So I go to sleep at 10:00 p.m., and oh, oh, I'm awoken by that banshee-sticking-that knife-in-my-left-thigh-again feeling, only this time level 11 pain. Sue comes into the bedroom and sees the same fluids again. I lay back down, and she calls the doctor. I roll over to my left side; I can hear and feel fluids going from the right side of my head across the top of my head and between the skin and skull to the left side of my head.

Sue says, "I see the fluids flowing across the top of your head."

Sue calls the doctor, we get his answer service, and the doctor calls back in five minutes. I told the doctor what had happened. He tells me to go to the emergency room immediately!

I go into surgery; they find that there is a bacterial infection on the skull fragment. So they threw away the skull fragment and replaced it with a titanium plate. Now I got a dent in my skull like I got hit in the head with a bowling ball. Recovery is a lot of fun; I have more tubes running in and out of me than a hopped-up engine in a hot rod. I had a drain on my left temple, my bladder, a pick line for antibiotics, and two spinal fluids on the upper and lower back.

I ask if I had a catheter, and my nurse says, "Yes, you do."

I demanded to have it removed because it made me have the urge to urinate constantly. My nurse resisted; why? Because they didn't want me to move at all. I understand now because when they removed the catheter for me to urinate, I needed to stand, so the nurses had to raise my drains for the spinal. Why? Because when the drains are too low for too long, I get a severe backache level of 10. So how do we get rid of the backache? Morphine. How to describe this? It gets rid of the pain, yes, but I started seeing some interesting things. First, there was a war going on in the streets outside, and I was close to getting ready to go outside and fight.

Fortunately, Sue brought me back to reality, thank God, because it seemed so real. Every day was a new adventure. Like I was seeing nurses making pullovers and shorts they had at their station; why? Because they were stealing patients' identities. I would hear that a patient died, then a nurse would go back into a room behind their station, then come out with the pullover and shorts that they had made; they had dyed their hair and assumed the dead patient's name. Thank God for Sandy, my daughter, and Sue, my wife; they convinced me that I was seeing things because I feared for my life. I had one nurse that was excellent; when I needed assistance to urinate, he was there to keep the spinal drains at the right height. I didn't need any morphine because I had no pain.

At the end of his shift, I could hear him thinking that he would not be having children to pass on his name, but then I noticed that it wasn't my ears that heard that, but my heart did, then I got the message to tell him that his son would be the next George Washington. So I got him to return to tell him, and he said, "Thank you!" I never saw him again.

The remainder of my stay in the recovery room stay was very uncomfortable because the nurse that I had was inattentive. She threatened to restrain me because I was not to move till she showed up when I buzzed for assistance. I told her I had to go bad, and I had waited a long time, several minutes, and she said I was not the only patient that she had and I needed to wait, or she was going to restrain me! Oh, I still remember her name, Maria. Anthony was an excellent nurse. So now I was back on the morphine trip because of the lack of attentiveness of Maria.

Now my room was moved again from hospital to house to another house, and I am being moved again back to the hospital because I am asking too many questions about my moves, but the room number never changes, number 24 on a sliding glass door. When I got back to the hospital, my doctor removed the spinal, and I moved to ICU. Almost immediately, I was discharged from the hospital, and when I get home, I started seeing things. First thing, I was resting in my lazy boy when I saw a herd of GEICO geckos crawling all over my wife, Sue. When one crawled onto her glasses and had no reaction, I realized that I was seeing something that wasn't there. So I ask Sue why are all those geckos crawling on her, and she says, "Where?"

That is when my granddaughter and Cassandra say, "There, there, and there." Boy did Sue get excited; the geckos disappeared. Next, I could see something hanging behind the coats on the coat rack on the wall, and it had a demonic red face with little horns. But when I saw the slats on the wooden floor starting to move, I knew that I was seeing things still. My older sister asked me later, "How do you like tripping like the hippies of the late sixties?"

I told her, "I did not like it at all."

My taste buds were still messed up, and I believed that my sense of smell and taste was disconnected. No matter what I tasted, it didn't taste as it tasted before. April and May were just sitting around the house and healing. I would sit and watch the world go by.

On the day of my release from the stroke, I knew that my left side had something wrong, so I thought, *Why not take a walk to the windows about twenty feet away?* I think well, a little unsteady, not quite as balanced as before, but I can deal with this. What? When I looked down from the eighth-story window, what I saw was a helicopter prop in idle rotation. They look like shadows coming out the side of the building, but their centers are inside the building across the alleyway. I thought, *If they are shadows, where is the shadow on top of the building?*

That was rather weird, so I called Sue over and asked her, "What do you see down there?"

She says, "What?" Well, that tells me that she couldn't see what I was looking at. Then I hear a little girl behind me, whining, "Where are my mommy and daddy?" But when I turn around from the window, what? I was looking at a little girl's shadow not on the floor or wall but standing next to me, about three feet away from me. I could see the spit curls down to her shoulder, and she was holding a doll in her right hand by arm. She was wearing a sleeveless dress down to just above her knees; she was crying, wanting to know where her mommy and daddy were. Then, I got this feeling in my chest, then I heard, "Her mother and father were killed in a car accident that she was injured in. She was flown in by helicopter, then she died a few days later, you are seeing her memories, send her to the light."

That is when the light appeared under the stairway, I saw her look at it, and I told her, "Your mommy and daddy were over there in the light." She walked toward the light, and when she got to the light, in a flash, she was like sucked into the light, and the light shrunk into nothing. She had found her parents again, and she had been there since the late 1950s (fifty-seven seems right). *Wow*, that was something different. Sue was standing behind me to my right, and the shadow figure was behind me to my left. Sue says, "Who are you talking to?"

I say, "Nobody."

When I got home, that's when things really got interesting. As I was sitting on the couch, I noticed two figures across the street. Immediately I knew it was the Bonny's; they had passed in the 1970s. Mr. Bonny passed from a leg operation first, then Mrs. Bonny passed from a car accident about a year later. Then I saw Steve walking around his van across the street, but he passed in August of 2010. That's when I noticed that I wasn't seeing with my eyes or hearing with my ears, and this was being seen and heard through the heart.

Not Again

February was a lot of doctor visits, light exercises, a lot of rest, and healing. It was rough because the back, neck, and shoulder injuries were making me tired all the time. I started going to bed at 10:00 p.m. On March 9, 2011, I was awoken by a pain in my left thigh on a scale from 1 to 10, and it registered a 10. When I sat up on the edge of the bed, I felt the moisture on my right forearm. I asked Sue, "Am I sweating?"

She said, "No, there is fluid coming out of this wound on the right side of my forehead."

She called my doctor the next morning, and he said to come on in. During the examination, my doctor did everything but stand me on my head, trying to get the fluids to flow with no luck. His conclusion was it was probable spinal fluids, and I was told to go home and rest.

Sue asks, "What if it happens again?"

He says, "Call me."

So I go to sleep at 10:00 p.m., and oh, oh, I'm awoken by that banshee-sticking-that knife-in-my-left-thigh-again feeling, only this time level 11 pain. Sue comes into the bedroom and sees the same fluids again. I lay back down, and she calls the doctor. I roll over to my left side; I can hear and feel fluids going from the right side of my head across the top of my head and between the skin and skull to the left side of my head.

Sue says, "I see the fluids flowing across the top of your head."

Sue calls the doctor, we get his answer service, and the doctor calls back in five minutes. I told the doctor what had happened. He tells me to go to the emergency room immediately!

I go into surgery; they find that there is a bacterial infection on the skull fragment. So they threw away the skull fragment and replaced it with a titanium plate. Now I got a dent in my skull like I got hit in the head with a bowling ball.

The Nightmare Begins

Recovery is a lot of fun; I have more tubes running in and out of me than a hopped-up engine in a hot rod. I had a drain on my left temple, my bladder, a pick line for antibiotics, and two spinal fluids on the upper and lower back.

I ask if I had a catheter, and my nurse says, "Yes, you do."

I demanded to have it removed because it made me have the urge to urinate constantly. My nurse resisted; why? Because they didn't want me to move at all. I understand now because when they removed the catheter for me to urinate, I needed to stand, so the nurses had to raise my drains for the spinal. Why? Because when the drains are too low for too long, I get a severe backache level of 10. So how do we get rid of the backache? Morphine. How to describe this? It gets rid of the pain, yes, but I started seeing some interesting things. First, there was a war going on in the streets outside, and I was close to getting ready to go outside and fight.

Fortunately, Sue brought me back to reality, thank God, because it seemed so real. Every day was a new adventure. Like I was seeing nurses making pullovers and shorts they had at their station; why? Because they were stealing patients' identities. I would hear that a patient died, then a nurse would go back into a room behind their station, then come out with the pullover and shorts that they had made; they had dyed their hair and assumed the dead patient's name. Thank God for Sandy, my daughter, and Sue, my wife; they convinced me that I was seeing things because I feared for my life. I had one nurse that was excellent; when I needed assistance to urinate, he was there to keep the spinal drains at the right height. I didn't need any morphine because I had no pain.

At the end of his shift, I could hear him thinking that he would not be having children to pass on his name, but then I noticed that it wasn't my ears that heard that, but my heart did, then I got the message to tell him that his son would be the next George Washington. So I got him to return to tell him, and he said, "Thank you!" I never saw him again.

The remainder of my stay in the recovery room stay was very uncomfortable because the nurse that I had was inattentive. She threatened to restrain me because I was not to move till she showed up when I buzzed for assistance. I told her I had to go bad, and I had waited a long time, several minutes, and she said I was not the only patient that she had, and I needed to wait, or she was going to restrain me! Oh, I still remember her name, Maria. Anthony was an excellent nurse. So now I was back on the morphine trip because of the lack of attentiveness of Maria.

The Nightmare Begins
(Continuation)

Now my room was moved again from hospital to house to another house, and I am being moved again back to the hospital because I am asking too many questions about my moves, but the room number never changes, number 24 on a sliding glass door. When I got back to the hospital, my doctor removed the spinal, and I moved to ICU. Almost immediately, I was discharged from the hospital, and when I get home, I started seeing things. First thing, I was resting in my lazy boy when I saw a herd of GEICO geckos crawling all over my wife, Sue. When one crawled onto her glasses and had no reaction, I realized that I was seeing something that wasn't there. So I ask Sue why are all those geckos crawling on her, and she says, "Where?"

That is when my granddaughter and Cassandra say, "There, there, and there." Boy did Sue get excited; the geckos disappeared. Next, I could see something hanging behind the coats on the coat rack on the wall, and it had a demonic red face with little horns. But when I saw the slats on the wooden floor starting to move, I knew that I was seeing things still. My older sister asked me later, "How do you like tripping like the hippies of the late sixties?"

I told her, "I did not like it at all."

Time to Heal

My taste buds were still messed up, and I believed that my sense of smell and taste was disconnected. No matter what I tasted, it didn't taste as it tasted before. April and May were just sitting around the house and healing. I would sit and watch the world go by.

My grandson was sitting for the first three months since the stroke. He was eating some potato chips that I liked, and I asked him for one. I put it in my mouth, and it didn't taste like the potato chips that I remembered, but it did taste like it was related to a potato. I couldn't believe that the potato chip that I had eaten since I was a child now tasted like something else. It tasted so bad that I spat it out immediately.

Now I understood why my weight was at 225 pounds, pretty good being that in the fall of 2009, I weighed as much as 280, and that is when I decided to lose some weight. I had dropped my weight to 257 prior to the car accident. I thought, *What a way to lose weight*, but I wouldn't recommend this diet to anyone. From April to June, I don't remember too much. Thanks to my grandchildren and wife, they had taken some pictures that were time dated, and it helped me recall what was going on while I was on some very heavy medication to prevent seizures, which, according to my new neurologist, I did not have one after they tested me. Some of the pictures were quite disturbing, seeing that the pouches that I had in my gown pockets were the drains from the tubes that were to the left temple that went under the skin across the top of my head to the right side of my head; *wow*.

June 2011

My taste buds and sense of smell were still not quite together yet, but a potato chip was beginning to taste almost like a potato chip, hoorah! So I decided it was time to go to a restaurant and see what I could taste. Sue and I went to a Ruby Tuesdays, so I ordered baby back ribs. While waiting for the order, oh, oh, I see and feel something very odd. I can see the right end of the salad bar, and I see like a mist about three feet tall, then I feel and hear in my head that it's a little girl. She is very happy because Mommy has taken her out to eat, and she really liked the salad bar. I tell Sue what I just saw. The next thing I know, I am seeing in my head the trunk of a white car opened, then I see a white hanky wrapped around a left hand coming from the left going over my nose and mouth. Now I'm seeing from the eyes of a mother, she is looking over at the Denny's to the right, and she sees a couple of people looking her way. Hurry put her in the trunk fast; she laid her on her back, and she grabbed the piece of duct tape and placed it over her mouth because she talked in her sleep.

Oh, oh, the couple were leaving the restaurant, and they were looking her way. Quick put the cap back on the bottle and put it in the trunk. She closes the trunk, gets in the car, starts the car, puts it in reverse, and leaves. Now I see in the trunk the little girl turned over from her back to her left side, and her right foot kicks the bottle over. The gagging was the worst part; I could feel being suffocated then sleep. Then back inside the car, Mommy thinks she smells something, pulls over, and opens the trunk. Oops, the smell was chloroform; she backs off and watches. *Is she breathing? No, she is not, oh well, I guess she is dead.* Mommy sees the garbage bag to the left of the little girl and reaches in, throws the bag over the little girl, closes the trunk, and continues to her boyfriend's house; I see her going to him. The last thing I see is the face of the individual that she went to see. My food has arrived, but I just look at my food. *Oh my gosh, what have I just seen!*

As Sue and I leave, I look to the left, and I can see the place where I saw the white car parked. I tell Sue we need to come back tomorrow to see if I can send the little girl onward. When we come back, I tell Sue where to park. We park and wait; I see this white kitten standing on the sidewalk at the corner of the building, looking at the restaurant next door, just like Mommy did. I see that Sue is looking to the right, and I tell her to look at that, pointing at the side of the building.

She says, "Look at what?" The kitten was gone; I told her what I saw, and we couldn't see a kitten or anything there. So we wait, but nothing is happening. After fifteen minutes, I notice some movement in the bush, and alas, the kitten is in the bush. I tell Sue, "Look!" Yes, we both see the kitten, then I feel it; that is the little girl's kitty, and she plays with the kitty. Two days later, Sue and I rode by because I wanted to look, and as we rode by the benches outside, I could feel her sitting there, waiting for Mommy. I've ridden by quite a bit since the last time; I felt her sitting on the bench, but I've not seen her again.

July to September

July and August were doing nothing but waiting to go to doctors and healing. While I was sitting in my lazy boy watching TV, I scanned through the channels and I came across the trial of Casey Anthony. There was the individual that Casey went to see, sitting in the crowd of people on the left, watching Casey on the right. So in the middle of July, my doctor tested me for seizures, and seeing that I had not any, he weaned me off the Keppra, which was to relax me, and it did. August 5 was my last dose, and did I feel more alert after this! My spinal injuries were still causing a lot of pain, but in everybody's life, a little rain will fall, and I will learn to live with it. Then I get the news that my mother has decided to give me and Sue the van; we are quite surprised. When my younger sister decided to go on a vacation to New Smyrna, we decided to visit them one evening. So we went out to eat, oh, oh, what is everything going to taste like? Very picky as usual now, I was used to eating anything but liver. As we rode back home, the feeling in my chest, yes? It's my father; he tells me that he went to Momma in her sleep and told her, "Think about giving the van to Sue and Ricky for being there for us," and "They really need it." I thanked Dad at that time because we needed it. In September, Sue and I looked forward to vacation to Kentucky and Pennsylvania.

We get permission to take Justin and Cassie with us, and now that I'm off the Keppra, my doctor tells me that I am not allowed to drive for six months after stopping the Keppra. I asked, "Why?"

He says, "You will probably have a seizure, and if you're driving, you might find yourself wrestling an alligator or hitting a five-year-old child."

Well, hitting the child was not something that I wanted to do, so no driving for six months. So Sue has to drive all of us to Kentucky to visit family and friends, then to Pennsylvania for the wedding of my goddaughter Melissa to Charles, then back to Florida. Oh boy! What an adventure that was, but that was successful.

In November and December, I got very lucky in bingo. I won the G-ball twice. I was told to give $300 for the endowment fund on the first one, then when I won the second one, I was told to give $200.

December

NEW MEXICO

So off to New Mexico Sue and I flew. What a trip! The flight was a little rough, but when we landed in Albuquerque, the plane got hit by a gust that picked the plane up about fifty feet and turned us ninety degrees clockwise. But the pilot turned it immediately counterclockwise and had set us down a little hard. It scared a lot of people, including Sue, but I thought it was fun! I have *God* on my side. I was enjoying the vacation, playing with my granddaughter and grandson. Around Christmas Day, we all had breakfast at Los Lunas; we were outside in the garden, and I noticed my daughter-in-law was gloomy, so I asked what was wrong. She said I put a memorial on Facebook about her brother's anniversary of passing and nobody reacted to it. She said she could see him up there, sitting back and watching on a seven-foot-screen TV the New Jersey Devils. Within minutes, I hear from above, "No, I'm not watching hockey, I'm watching all of you!" I repeated what I heard. I heard from somebody in the group that he'd talk to me before he talks to you. Hence, I was very careful about talking to too many people.

January

BAD BOY 2012

February

ROAD TRIPS

Yeah! I can now drive. So I am going to be grandpa sat by Justin and Cassie from Tuesday to Thursday, so I going to show Cassie and Justin Florida. My first trip was to Sebastian Inlet; boy, the changes, I believe, it had been twenty years since I've been here. It is now a state park that you now have to pay to park there. They have a museum on the south side, and I swear I saw some of my fishing lures there. I used to fish after midnight on full moon nights, and I think that is going to be difficult now. The next trip was going to be Ponce Inlet Lighthouse at South Daytona Beach.

As soon as I got to the lighthouse property, I could feel him at the top of the lighthouse. So I figured that I would send him onward. I have never climbed to the top of a lighthouse, fire tower, or any stairs past three stories, and I was scared of heights. But since I worked in a warehouse and worked on a high picker, I am no longer scared of heights. Because I was going up to meet this spirit, I got to the last window from the top, about ten stories, and that's when he attacked. First, I got a pain on the left side of my head like a hand squeezing it, then my back started hurting in the small of my back like a thumb digging into it, also, at the base of my neck on the right side, a finger was digging into the herniation there. Then my knees started buckling, *Oh no, am I having another stroke?* Then I see and hear him inside my head, "I'm not going anywhere, you are going to leave here now!"

He looked Spanish, about five foot seven slim with black hair, a very short beard, and a mustache, looking down, pointing, and yelling at me. He was wearing light-colored pants with suspenders and a plaid shirt. I went back down, still wondering if I was having a stroke. I get out of the lighthouse, and I see a bench to my left; I walk over and sit down. The pain is not as bad, but it is still there. So after about twenty minutes, Cassie and Justin come out of the lighthouse. I tell them it is time to go home because there is something wrong with me.

I still feel the pain, so we go out to the van; we leave the property and head for home, but as soon as we get on A1A, the pain vanishes immediately. And then I get that feeling in my chest, and I'm told, "He can't hurt me anymore, I'm out of his territory." Not going home now; we ride north on A1A till we get to Palm Coast, and we stop at a restaurant and have a late lunch. We returned home about two hours after the lighthouse, and the pain must have been caused by the entity at the lighthouse because I do not feel that pain again.

St. Augustine

The following week, I decided that it was time to take Cassie and Justin to the lighthouse and castle in St. Augustine because I had promised them that they needed to see the real history of Florida. We went to the castle first, then the theater, then examined the castle, but when we got to the room in the left corner of the castle from the entrance, I got that feeling, and then I saw him; he was about thirty-five years old, wearing a white sailor uniform; he was asking, "Why am I being executed?" Then *boom*, *boom*, I feel the pound-stabbing pain in the chest, twice from being shot. I had to go to see if I could see anything at the lighthouse that was supposed to be haunted. As soon as I got on the property, I could feel something, but it was very weak compared to Ponce Inlet. I followed where I thought it was coming from, and it led me to the lighthouse.

Still, I wasn't sure where I was being led, and alas, I found myself compelled to go into the house attached to the lighthouse. Cassie and Justin were following, and we checked out the house; then I felt that she was up there, along the steps to the top of the lighthouse. Oh boy, I had tried to climb these steps about thirty to thirty-five years before, but I only made it to the second level because I was scared of heights. I needed to climb, but Justin and Cassie led the way. The climb was easy because you climb about twenty-four steps, then you have a landing about fifteen inches long to rest to make the next climb of twenty-four steps. The next thing I knew, I was on the third level, and everything was fine, but I still felt she was up higher.

Just as I am about to get to the fourth level, three steps before, I get that feeling in my chest, then I felt the shake of fear, I felt the fear in the little girl about eight to nine years old, and I could hear her, and she said, "I'm so scared up here, I need to go down, but I can't

25

do it." I started to go up to her, but after four steps, I felt like there was more here, and I needed to go back down, but I didn't want what happened at Ponce Inlet to happen here. I get outside, and I speak to one of the employees working at a kiosk and ask her if a little girl had died here in the past. She tells me that there were two girls, twelve and fifteen, that had an accident where a cart had fallen on them, crushing them to death. I told her, "No, there had to be a girl that was younger than that."

She then said, "There was a younger girl, about nine years old, that drowned in the same accident." That had to be her; I was certain. Days later, I'm still wondering why she is still up there, and I'm told that she was a slave girl, and she had to go up there to help unload the cart when it arrived.

October 2013

Sue and I are eating out at an Irish Pub in Winter Garden when I hear, "Hi, I'm Paul, your great-great-great-great-great grandfather that married your Indian squaw grandmother." The next day I'm getting exercise, walking around the world showcase at Epcot, and I'm directed toward the Irish kiosk. Paul told me to try the Irish mead wine, which was very pleasant. Then he tells me his name is Paul Jervis.

Paul did a lot of communicating with me from October to January. He showed me when he was released from the dungeon in Ireland the last time, where the magistrate told him that he better get out of town or he was going to get buried over there, pointing at a spot under a shade tree. Paul thought, *No problem*, went down to the docks, and caught a ride to the Americas. He ended up in the Carolinas, where he met up with Omawogee. She was a Cherokee squaw that was a great hunter, and Paul was a good cook. Omawogee would bring her catch to Paul; he would cook it, then sell it to the village. And, of course, they got married, and Omawogee changed her name to Mae. That way, the villagers could pronounce her name.

Now I understand my mother, Nella Mae, Aunt Mae, and Grandma Rose Mae. When I told my sisters about Paul Jervis, they told me that the Indian squaw was from the Tischendorf side, grandma Rose Mae Jervis (Tischendorf).

After I found this out, I asked, "Paul, how?" He told me his great-great-granddaughter married a Tischendorf. I asked, "Were you related to John C. Jervis?"

He said, "No, different clan."

March 2014

Oh boy, we are going to EPCOT to watch ELO perform. Twenty minutes into the performance, I get that feeling in my chest before I get my visions. All of a sudden, I saw yellow flowers moving right to left, but I saw them through a pair of binoculars in a helicopter. Now I see a .50 caliber machine gun in front of me. I'm the left gunner. Then I hear in my head, "All right, listening to ELO out on the runs, be killing some Gook"; the person laughs. I thought, *Where is this going?* When *bang, bang, bang, bang!* I feel four shots; first, in the right ball socket, next, on the right shoulder, then the left shoulder, and finally on the left ball socket. Angel says the right shoulder had a fragment ricochet through the aorta, and he bled out instantly. Then this spirit that was in my head asked me to tell this woman sitting two seats in front of me that he was still watching over her. There was no way that I could tell these people when this happened because these visions are very emotional, and I am bawling like a baby.

October 2014

Now I was at my drugstore getting my medicine when an angel told me that the gentleman, sitting partially behind that plant, to talk to him about his sciatica problem like mine. So I go over and say, "You look like you have a sciatica problem like mine."

He asks, "How do you know about my problem?"

After a little chitchat, my angel says to tell him about that helicopter incident; I do, and he commits, "My father died on the helicopter to evacuate. Okay, my medicine is ready. Bye."

As I leave the store, my angel says, "Yes, that was his father."

Now my life is that I get messages from above at any time through dreams, usually nightmares that are unpleasant. One morning, I was awoken by a dream where I was at day care at a house that had a play yard in the middle. It looks like a party with a lot of boys and girls. I'm seeing this through the eyes of a little boy, and he's on the south side of this yard, seeing the girls going to the north side where this older man is getting the girls to line up in front of him. One by one, the girls stand in front of the man with happy and sad expressions. Now I see why! He is having the little girls petting his penis! Later, I was watching the news, and there was a picture of that man accused of molestation at day care. Oh, yes, he is guilty!

I was sitting and talking to a bank manager when all of a sudden, I saw this middle-aged woman yelling at this man outside the bank at night. "That's all she could get out of the ATM." Next, he slashed her with a machete, and I get to feel what she felt. The first two were the worst because I think she was dead after the second.

2022

I still receive messages. When I turn on the news, I'm usually not too surprised at what I see.

About the Author

Richard Mitchell was born on May 14, 1950, and raised in Louisville, Kentucky, the third child of four, his mother and father, Nella and Howard Mitchell. Richard met the love of his life in TV and English class in 1966, Sue Frances Meyer. They were married on May 2, 1969. Their twin sons were born on May 16, 1970, then their daughter was born on February 19, 1973. Now they have three grandsons, two granddaughters, and two great-granddaughters. They were only seventy-two. His work history started when he was an eleven-year-old paperboy. When he was sixteen years old, he tried Burger King for a couple of months, then worked stockroom of Ben Synder's until Sue and Richard packed up and moved to Winter Park, Florida.

Richard started working at the check printers; John Harland worked there from 1969 to 1975. He started as a janitor and left there as a printer. On December 11, 1975, Walt Disney World needed a press operator. Richard was hired to start the printing and numbering of passports to eliminate the ABCDE ticket books. He was told that he saved WDW $40,000 in the first month successfully. He stayed until affirmed action put a man in charge of my ticket department, left Disney on September 26, 1986, to the outside printshop. Then Xerox killed the printshops on May 23, 1989, and Richard was back to Disney as a truck driver and finished up working warehouses until he retired on October 20, 2012.